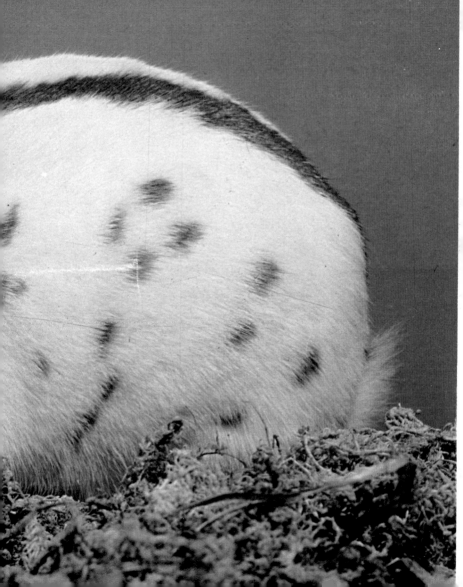

This is a fine specimen of a tan English spot. As the name implies, widely spaced dark spots on a light background are characteristic of this variety. Photo by M. Gilroy.

Contents

A Beginner's Guide To
Rabbits

Written By
Paul Wimner

Introduction

Contrary to popular belief, rabbits are not rodents but belong to the mammalian order Lagomorpha, which also includes hares and pikas. Although there are definite similarities between lagomorphs and rodents, for example, chisel-like incisor teeth, there are differences that necessitate classification in two different orders.

There are many different species of rabbit and hare, most of which are native to the great land masses of the Northern Hemisphere. However, the species which was forefather to all of our present domestic breeds is the Common European Rabbit (*Oryctolagus cuniculus*). In the wild the species is a dull grey-brown in colour and may reach three to four pounds in weight when adult. It is believed to have originated in Southern Europe, possibly upon the Iberian Peninsula, from whence it was transported by early travellers to all parts of the continent. It is still a very common animal in Europe in spite of the continuing war waged against it by farmers, landowners, and gamekeepers.

In more recent times the disease virus Myxomatosis, which was isolated from a species of wild South American lagomorph, was developed in Australia to combat the large population of feral European Rabbits which had resulted from the introduction of that species to the continent in the year 1859. The same disease was later intentionally introduced into Britain, and although it seemed to have a drastic effect on the rabbit population at first the prolific animals soon developed a certain amount of immunity to it and wild rabbits now appear to be as common as ever.

Economically rabbits are quite important. During times of national meat shortages, particularly during and directly following the two world wars, they have been a major source of fresh protein. Indeed, breeds like the Flemish Giant and the New Zealand White were specially developed for meat production.

The fur of the rabbit has also been widely exploited and breeds like the Chinchilla Rabbit have been evolved to supply a market for good furs. Rabbit wool is another relatively new industry. The

autiful Angora Rabbit can produce up to twelve ounces of first
ade wool each year and the good point here is that the rabbit does
t have to be slaughtered.

folklore the rabbit has played many important roles, the most
nous being the "Easter Bunny". This legend is thought to have
iginated with our Germanic ancestors who believed that the "Eas-
Hare" was transformed from a bird by Ostara, the Goddess of
ring. Legend has it that forever after the Easter Bunny lays eggs
the spring. In Germany the "Easter Bunny" is still known as the
)sterhase". To this day children of many European countries go
o their gardens early on the morning of Easter Sunday to search
r the eggs of the "Easter Hare" which have been secretly con-
aled there the evening before by their parents.

more recent times the rabbit has become the major character in
any children's stories. Who has not heard of Br'er Rabbit, Peter
ttontail, or Bugs Bunny? In fact, the rabbit has played an impor-
it role in the teaching of children.

ne of the author's earliest pets as a child was a large buck rabbit
no particular variety who was called "Big Ears". He lived in a
rden shed which he shared with fourteen guinea pigs, several
dgerigars, a grass snake, and a jackdaw. Big Ears was a charcter
vill never forget. He would be let out on the lawn with the guinea
gs and he would appear to be their leader and protector. I re-
ember one day, when a neighbour's cat had been stalking one of
e guinea pigs, that Big Ears ambled casually up to the cat, turned
s back on it, and then leapt suddenly into the air and hit the cat a
ow full in the face with both of his hind feet. A look of complete
tonishment appeared on the cat's face before it turned and bolted
ck over the fence never to return to our garden, at least not when
g Ears was around.

g Ears was with us for many years before I developed a more ma-
re interest in breeding fancy rabbits and I am sure that he played
major part in my wanting to learn more about all types of
imals.

1.
Varieties

There are more than fifty varieties of rabbits ranging in size from the eleven to fourteen pound Flemish Giant to the two to three pound Netherland Dwarf. Many of the breeds were first developed for an express purpose, such as meat or pelt production. However, most of the smaller, more modern types were developed solely for exhibition or ornamental purposes, or just for suitability as pets. Let us look at some of the breeds, starting with the older varieties.

Above: *A dwarf lop, one of the more popular rabbit varieties. Photo by R. Hanson.*
Facing page: *Though bred selectively for centuries, some domestic rabbits still resemble their wild ancestors in overall form and color.*

Flemish Giant

The Flemish Giant is the largest of all the domestic breeds and an adult can weigh between eleven and fourteen pounds. As it is such a large rabbit, it should be kept only by those who have space in which to build large hutches and the time and funds to provide great quantities of food. This breed has been popular in the past for both meat and pelt production and is today one of the major exhibition varieties. Fanciers try to breed their specimens as large and as heavy as possible.

The colour of the Flemish Giant should be dark grey finely flecked all over with black. The ears should be large and erect. These rabbits are intelligent and I have known some individual specimens to be moody; one particular buck would kick and bite at every opportunity. However, most of them if given plenty of attention will make the most affectionate of pets.

Belgian Hares

As its name implies, the Belgian Hare is similar in appearance to a hare, both in size and in shape. A large, lanky body with long legs and ears make it one of the "racers" of the fancy. Specimens may weigh up to nine pounds and are normally beautiful chestnut in colour. This breed requires plenty of exercise to keep it trim and should therefore have regular access to outside runs.

English

The English Rabbit is one of the more attractive of the fancy breeds. The most popular colouring is black and white, but other colours including grey and white, chocolate and white, and blue and white are available. The ground is white and the darker colour covers the nose, eyes, and ears, extending into a narrow blotchy line down the spine and appearing as small spots on other parts of the body. It is a medium sized rabbit weighing about seven pounds when adult. It is very hardy and a good breeder, the young growing rapidly. It is docile and makes an excellent pet.

Himalayan

Another attractive medium-sized rabbit, the Himalayan is usually white with red eyes and black nose, ears, feet and tail, although other colours are occasionally available. It is thought that this variety originated in China. It is a smaller breed than the English, weighing about five pounds, but it is similar in temperament.

Dutch

The Dutch variety is probably the most widely kept of all the fancy breeds. It is a small, pretty rabbit which has a set of typical markings, a white saddle with rear end and head markings of black, tan, blue, chocolate or grey. Rarely weighing more than five pounds, the Dutch Rabbit is a good breeder and the does are excellent mothers. These rabbits make good all-around pets.

The Dutch rabbit is a very attractive variety, and while no two have exactly the same pattern, the symmetry of the white and black markings is very important.

Old English Lop

The Lop is one of our oldest varieties. It is a heavy rabbit, weighing up to ten pounds, and it has extremely long, wide ears which hang down the side of the head and touch the floor, hence the name "Lop". The usual colour is fawn, but fawn and white, black and white, and tortoiseshell and white are occasionally to be seen. The Lop is not a very active rabbit and does not require a great deal of exercise, but care must be taken that it is not overfed as it is prone to acquiring fat very quickly.

This rabbit is a pleasing soft tan color on the back, fading to gray on head and underside.

Silver

Another old breed, these medium-sized rabbits of five or six pounds in weight are available in three colours: silver-grey, brown, and fawn.

Netherland Dwarf

The smallest of all rabbits, the Netherland Dwarf is little larger than a guinea pig and in fact the two animals can be housed together. The Netherland Dwarf comes in almost every colour or combination of colours imaginable. An extremely short-eared variety weighing only about two pounds, the breed is very popular as a pet.

Polish

Another small rabbit weighing two to three pounds, the Polish is a white breed which may have blue or red eyes. In spite of its appealing looks, it is not an easy breeder and is therefore not recommended for the beginner.

Tan

Black and Tan, Blue and Tan, Lilac and Tan, and Chocolate and Tan are the colours available, the tan colour being on the underside of the chin and body and also around the rims of the ears. This breed is one of the author's favourites and good specimens have a most wonderful sheen to their coats. An adult Tan rabbit weighs about four pounds.

Argenté

The Argenté varieties originated in France and come in the following colours and sizes. The Argenté de Champagne is a blue-haired, silver tipped variety, weighing eight or nine pounds. The Argenté Bleu is a lavender-haired, silver tipped variety weighing about six pounds. The Argenté Creme is a cream coloured rabbit with orange highlights weighing about five pounds. The Argenté Brun sports various tones of brown to make up an extremely beautiful coat, the adult rabbit weighing approximately six pounds.

New Zealand

These rabbits of eight or nine pounds in weight are usually white or brick-red in colour. The breed contrary to its name is in fact American.

Chinchilla

Originally developed as a fur breed, the Chinchilla has one of the finest coats of all rabbits. The soft grey and blue pelt resembles real chinchilla in both colour and texture. These rabbits are docile and make cuddly pets. The Chinchilla rabbit weighs up to six pounds but a larger version called the Chinchilla Giganta is occasionally available.

Beveren

The Beveren is a large rabbit of seven to eight pounds which was developed in Belgium as a meat and pelt producer at the turn of the century. It is available in four colours, pure black, pure white, pure brown, and pure lavender.

Silver Fox

Named after the fox because its fur is said to resemble a fox's, the Silver Fox Rabbit is available in four colour varieties, black, blue, lilac, and chocolate. Each colour should be ticked with longer white hairs. An adult Silver Fox weighs between five and seven pounds.

Beaver

A large rabbit, weighing about nine pounds, the Beaver is named after the animal whose coat its own fur resembles.

Rex Rabbits

A Rex Rabbit is one in which the stiff guard hairs have been bred out, leaving an extremely short, soft coat which was developed as a valuable pelt breed in the early part of this century. Most of the breeds already described are available in Rex form, the most popular ones being Black, Blue, Lilac, Brown, Chinchilla, Sable, Tan, Himalayan, English, Californian, and Dutch.

There really is a rabbit under all that fuzz! The bizarre but beautiful angora rabbit is sometimes bred on farms for its fur, which is sheared periodically without harming the animal. Angoras make fine pets, but demand careful grooming to prevent matting of their fur.

Californian

This large rabbit is one of the newer breeds. It weighs approximately eight to ten pounds and with its dark ears, feet, nose, and tail it looks like a very large Himalayan Rabbit.

Havana

This is a medium-sized rabbit with a rich chocolate coat having a purplish sheen.

Lilac

This is a medium-sized rabbit which should weigh between five and a half to seven pounds. It is very attractive with soft pinkish grey fur.

Sable

These rabbits have very handsome fur coats. They were developed from the Chinchilla breed and weigh between five and seven pounds.

Satin

This rabbit possesses very velvety fur and is available in over twenty different colours. It weighs between six to eight pounds.

Siberian

This British breed was first developed in the 1930's. It is now available in brown, black, blue, and lilac varieties weighing from five to seven pounds.

Smoke Pearl

The coat of this very attractive rabbit shades from grey to pearl. It weighs from five to seven pounds.

Harlequin

This rabbit is very deserving of its name. Its fur is four very distinct colours arranged in a patchwork. There are different colours on each ear which reverse on the face. The body is covered with distinct rings and the front feet are each different colours with the hind feet behind the same colours reversed. This is a very difficult variety to breed and requires true dedication.

Angora

There are many other breeds of rabbit and it is impossible to describe them all in a volume of this size. There is however, one breed which deserves special attention - the *Angora*. This is one of the strangest but most beautiful phenomenons in the rabbit world. A well kept Angora has one of the finest and softest coats one can imagine but it will require much more attention than that of any other rabbit and must be thoroughly groomed at least once a month if the wool is not to become matted and knotted.

Angoras are still kept commercially in many parts of the world and garments manufactured from Angora Wool are much sought after and usually expensive. The wool yielding rabbits are often kept singly in small hutches with a wire floor to prevent the droppings from soiling the coat. The rabbits are sheared about four times a year and a good animal will supply about twelve ounces of wool per annum. The most popular colour variety is white, but they do come in other colours including Chinchilla, Golden, and Smoky.

A pet Angora Rabbit can be kept in a smaller hutch than many of the other varieties because, although it is a fairly large breed weighing six to eight pounds, it is a rather inactive one and spends hours sitting in one position. It is very easy to overfeed an Angora and they soon put on large quantities of fat if one is not careful. It is advisable to supply Angoras with more green food than other breeds as this helps to keep their long wool in prime condition.

Pet Angoras should be clipped at least once per year, preferably in the summer months or else a partial moulting will occur which not only causes intense matting of the fur but can also be extremely irritating to the rabbit. Often this results in a general deterioration in health and sickness caused by the rabbit pulling out its own coat and eating it. Before clipping the animal should be thoroughly groomed with a comb or brush and a parting made on the line of the spinal ridge. Sharp hairdressing scissors may be used and the wool should be clipped to within half an inch of the skin but not closer. It is best for two people to perform the operation, one to hold the rabbit and the other to clip it. When clipping the belly of a doe rabbit, particularly if pregnant, one should keep a sharp watch for the teats which could be clipped accidentally.

2.
Housing

Most breeds of rabbit are extremely hardy and will live without heat through the coldest of winters if they are provided with draught-free and waterproof quarters, dry bedding, and a balanced diet.

Red rabbits such as this one are comparatively rare. Perpetuating rare strains is always a challenge to the breeder.

Above: *Commercially built small animal cages are quite suitable for rabbits and are usually very easy to clean. Such cages are ideal for rabbits kept indoors as pets.* **Below:** *Outdoor rabbit hutches must be constructed carefully to provide adequate protection from the elements. Photo by M. Cummings.*

A group of different types of dwarf rabbits. Photo by R. Hanson.

There are many types of hutches that can be used for rabbits, and here again it is up to the individual as to what type of hutch he chooses. If the rabbits are to be kept indoors the metal framed, wire covered, laboratory type cages may be used.

Some of the types of rabbit housing the author has designed and constructed in the past will be described here. Each is selected for its practical as well as ornamental properties. Sizes are given for medium-sized rabbits such as Dutch, English, or Himalayan, and may be altered to accommodate larger or smaller breeds or to suit the particular whims of the fancier.

Single Rabbit Hutch

These are suitable for a single pet rabbit or for animals from larger breeding colonies which have to be kept separately, i.e. bucks separated from does.

Above: *These commercial cages are quite serviceable rabbit homes. Photo by M. Gilroy.*
Facing page: *At first glance this rabbit may appear to be of the Dutch variety, but is actually quite different, as it has longer fur and even facial markings. It is, however, a very pretty animal.*

This rabbit is kept in a cage with a wire mesh floor designed for easy cleaning. Many pet shops have cages such as these available.

For an outside hutch the following size is recommended: Length 1 m (3 1/2 ft), breadth 45 cm (18 in), height at front 50 cm (20 in), height at rear 45 cm (18 in). The most lasting and attractive material for construction is tongued and grooved cedarwood boarding mounted on 3 cm (1 1/4 in) x3 cm (1 1/4 in) soft timber framing, but to economise, the back, floor, and roof may be made from 10 or 12 mm (1/2 in) plywood.

Finally, for an outside hutch the roof must be covered with a good grade roofing felt which should be folded down over the edges of the roof and attached from the underside. Quite often it is possible to continue the felt from the roof right down the back of the hutch to give added protection.

The siting of an outside hutch is important. It should be placed on a stand at least 60 cm (2 ft) from the ground to discourage rats and mice from nesting underneath it, a situation which is certainly not desirable as these rodents carry diseases. The hutch should be placed in a sheltered position but one in which the sun can shine into the open part of it for at least some of the day. Even rabbits like to sunbathe and there is evidence that sunlight does them a certain amount of good.

During severe weather, particularly at night, the front of the hutch can be covered with burlap, attached by four nails to the top of the hutch and a couple of cup hooks at the bottom. The sacking can be unhooked at the bottom and folded over the top of the cage during the day.

Some rabbits have no housing worries—because they have no houses! Unlike some domestic varieties, this wild European rabbit (Oryctolagus cuniculus) *is quite able to deal with inclement weather conditions.*

There are many types of dwarf rabbits being bred, but most are characterized by their blunt, rounded faces and short ears. Photo by M. Gilroy.

Breeding Hutches

A breeding hutch should be similar in design to the single rabbit hutch but a little larger and with a few modifications. A good size for a breeding hutch for medium-sized rabbits would be 120 cm (47 in) long x 60 cm (23 in) deep x 55 cm (22 in) high at the front and 50 cm (20 in) at the back. One third of it should again be used as nesting quarters and a removable safety plank, about 10 cm (4 in) wide, is placed at the bottom of this just inside the door. This helps to stop the bedding and also young rabbits from falling out when the door is opened.

To prevent mother rabbit from being over-suckled by her youngsters it is advisable to fit a rest platform for her about 20 cm (8 in) from the base of the hutch. The platform can be about 15 cm (6 in) wide for a medium-sized doe and she can get up on it out of the way if she needs a rest from the litter.

If several breeding females are to be kept, a battery of breeding hutches may be constructed which may contain three or six units. A frame is made to take the required size and number of hutches, preferably from stout timber approximately 5 cm (2 in) x 7 1/2 cm

(3 in). More than three tiers of hutches are not recommended as servicing would then become too difficult.

The Morant Hutch

A popular type of rabbit hutch is one in which rabbits can graze directly from a lawn or other grassy patch. The Morant hutch, invented by Major G. Morant towards the end of the last century, is one such construction. It consists basically of a triangular arc, two thirds of which is covered with wire netting, the remaining third being a covered house. The whole of the floor is also covered with wire netting to stop the rabbits from burrowing out but enabling them to graze from the grass upon which the hutch is resting. To prevent fouling of any particular area the hutch should be moved daily to a new patch.

Although this type of hutch is normally in use only during the warmer parts of the year, it does help to cut down on the food bill, gives the animals more interest in being able to forage for their own food and certainly helps to improve the health of the inhabitants.

A Polish rabbit. Photo by M. Cummings.

A good-sized Morant hutch is about 150 cm (59 in) in length and 80 cm (32 in) high at the apex. The house should take up 50 cm (20 in) of the length and should be covered with tongued and grooved weather boarding. Inside the house a raised shelf should be fitted to enable the rabbits to sleep on a dry surface should they so wish. As this type of hutch is meant to be easily transportable it should not be made too heavy and the framework should be constructed of fairly light battens, say 3 cm (1 1/4 in) x 3 cm (1 1/4 in). The easiest way to make a Morant hutch is to make three frames of the correct size, and then join them with small triangular pieces of ply. However, a neater frame is produced when one takes the trouble to joint it properly.

The Colony Pen

One of the most interesting ways of keeping rabbits, if one has the space, is the colony system of allowing one buck to run with several does in a large open-air pen, something similar to a chicken run. The ambitious fancier can construct something which is quite elaborate and ornamental, shrubs and creepers can be grown in strategic positions around the pen and the weather-proof nesting quarters can be built to resemble an Alpine villa or even a Chinese pagoda. The house should be set on a concrete base and separate nesting boxes should be placed inside for the buck and each doe. In very bad weather the animals can be locked into the house. Care should be taken in the construction of the house to see that all parts are easily accessible for cleaning purposes, and that no superfluous niches are left for the benefit of mice or rats.

The outer pen should have a wire netting wall about 2 m (6 1/2 ft) high, the top 30 cm (1 ft) of which should be angled out to prevent the entry of cats and other predators. The base of the wire should be bent inwards for about 60 cm (2 ft) to prevent the rabbits from burrowing out. Once the initial grass has been destroyed by the rabbits the floor of the pen can be covered with sand which may be replaced as necessary. The size of the run depends on the number of rabbits to be kept and the amount of available space, but as a general guideline a pen 4 m (13 ft) x 2 m (6 1/2 ft) should be adequate for one buck and eight does.

3.
Feeding

As with all animals, including humans, it is important that captive rabbits receive a balanced diet; that is, balanced specifically for the rabbit as different animals require different balances. For instance, it would be rather stupid to feed cat food to a rabbit. A rabbit is a specialized mammal in its own way, it has evolved its own unique

Although photographed against a woodland backdrop,
this is not a wild rabbit. The Siamese sable rabbit is
a domestic breed.

method of digesting the types of food that are readily available to it in the wild. Therefore, to keep in the best of health the rabbit must have the correct ingredients in the proper proportions in its diet.

What then is a balanced diet? It is the variety and quantity of constituents required to maintain an animal in the best of physical and mental health. Basically, all animals need proteins, carbohydrates, fats, vitamins, minerals, and water in varying quantities depending on the animal. Before working out a balanced diet for a rabbit let us look at each of these constituents and consider how important they are.

Proteins are an important part of the diet of any animal as they are an integral part of muscle and tissue, important in the growth, replacement, and repair of worn out or damaged tissue. As rabbits are herbivorous, they are unable to digest first-class protein as in meat, so they must extract second-class protein from vegetation and process this into first-class protein for use in their own bodies. Vegetable proteins are found mainly in seed and grain and to a lesser extent in root crops and hay.

Carbohydrates, including starches and sugars, are necessary to provide energy and heat. The largest part of a rabbit's diet should consist of carbohydrates. They are found in nearly every ingredient which rabbits eat in the wild.

Fats also help to keep the animal warm and act as a food reserve should times become difficult or should extra energy be required at any time. Excess carbohydrate is converted into fats and this can be reconverted as and when necessary.

Vitamins are found in varying amounts in grain and in fresh greens, as are mineral salts.

Finally, the importance of fresh water must never be overlooked, for without it all of the rest of the diet would be useless. This can be supplied either in a heavy bowl that is not easily overturned or from a water dripper, an inverted glass bottle with a metal tube extending from the bottom.

Nowadays it is possible to buy a balanced rabbit diet in pellet form, usually known as rabbit pellets. These are manufactured from compressed mixtures of ground hay, straw, grain, fishmeal, and various

White rabbits have been popular for many years (probably due in no small part to Lewis Carroll). Actually, true white rabbits are albinos. Technically, an albino is an organism lacking black pigment (melanin), though frequently albinos lack all pigment and thus have the snow-white color of the rabbit shown here. The eye appears red because of blood flowing through its vessels (the eye itself is colorless in albinos). Photo by H. J. Richter.

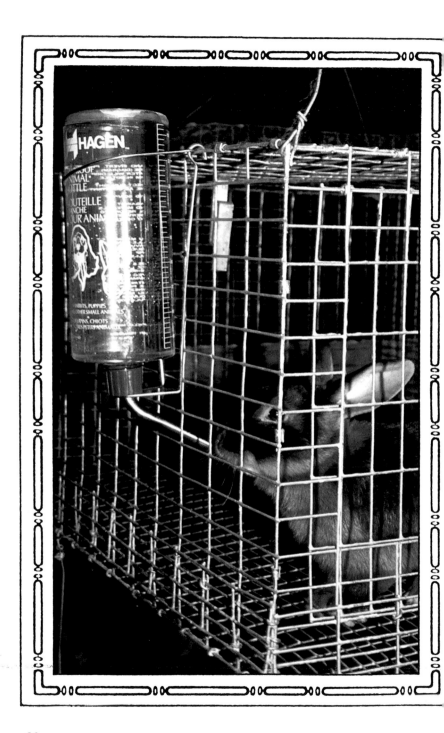

Above: This pretty little rabbit is the product of a cross between a white ermine rabbit and a marten-colored rabbit. *Below:* This is an orange rex rabbit, which has a color pattern much like that of many wild rabbits. *Facing page:* All rabbits require plenty of clean, fresh water. Commercial water bottles such as that shown are far superior to standing water in a dish, which is easily contaminated. Photo by V. Serbin.

other foods. The correct amount of vitamins and mineral salts are added and, theoretically, these pellets plus water are all a rabbit requires to keep in the best of physical health. However, if we want to give the poor fellow a little extra interest in life then a more varied diet should be given. By all means use rabbit pellets as a supplement to other foods. A fistful per rabbit per day should be ample.

The most interesting way to feed rabbits is to make up little menus, each one containing the correct constituents but varying in ingredients. For a medium-sized rabbit the following specimen menus are provided.

MORNING
Menu A
1 oz crushed oats
4 oz pellets
 3 oz roots (carrots, turnips, etc.)
Menu B
2 oz brown bread
2 oz wheat
4 oz greenfood
EVENING
Menu A
4 oz greenfood
4 oz hay
Menu B
4 oz hay
3 oz pellets
1 oz roots

The Brittania petite is a fairly small, slim breed. This one has a "smoke pearl" color. Photo by R. Hanson.

Fresh water, of course, should be available at all times.

It can be seen that there is no end to the variety of menus one can prepare, especially during the summer months when so many greenfoods are available. The rabbit keeper with a garden can perhaps spare a plot for growing some of his own greenfoods for his rabbits and thereby save a little money. Many of the offcuts from domestic vegetables can also be used to feed rabbits, but they must be washed just as thoroughly as vegetables are for human consumption. The green and root crops suitable for rabbits are almost unlimited, but the following list will give a general guide as to what to grow.

Beetroot, broccoli, brussels sprouts, cabbage, carrots, cauliflower, celery, chicory, kale, kohlrabi, leek, lettuce, mangel-wurzels, parsnips, peas (including pods and foliage), turnips.

Wild greens are also useful and there is virtually no limit to the quantity and variety the rabbit fancier can collect during the summer months. There are, however, two dangers of collecting wild greens. If collected too close to highways or public footpaths there is a danger of contamination by vehicle fumes or by dogs, and there is also the added danger of inadvertently plucking some poisonous foliage along with the food item. Great care should therefore be taken when collecting wild greens .

Like many animals, rabbits enjoy a salt lick. Salt spools are available that attach easily to the insides of cages.

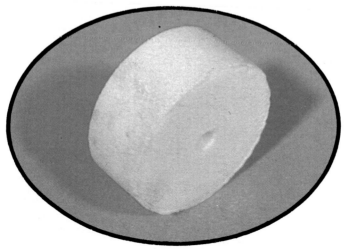

4.
Care

One of the most important aspects of keeping any captive animal in the best of health is the regular and thorough cleaning of the animal's quarters. In other words, the animal should be kept in hygienic conditions. The word hygiene means the science of the prevention and control of disease and that is exactly what we are trying to do. A rabbit which is well fed and kept in a clean, dry hutch will

*Above: The seal point Netherland dwarf has a snout that shades darker towards the tip. Photo by R. Hanson. **Facing page:** Wild rabbits are very alert animals that are easily startled and are quick to flee as danger approaches.*

No, this is not a dalmatian dog—look at the ears! This beautiful rex rabbit has a spotted pattern on the forward half of the body, but the pattern solidifies to nearly solid black on the hindquarters.

do much better than one whose accommodation is rarely cleaned. It will have a much higher level of resistance to disease and will also be in better mental health. Even rabbits can become neurotic if kept in the wrong conditions!

All rabbits should be groomed regularly to keep their fur in good condition and to accustom them to being handled. A good brushing should be given at least once a week and this will give you the opportunity of thoroughly inspecting the individuals for any signs of injury or disease.

Hutches should be cleaned out as often as possible and certainly not less than twice per week. It will be found that rabbits are creatures of habit and will usually pass droppings and urinate in one particular corner of the hutch. A good practice is to clean out the hutch thoroughly twice per week and on the other days clean out only the soiled corner. It is advisable to cover the hutch floor with a good absorbent material such as wood shavings, sawdust, or peat moss. The former is probably the most readily available and many carpentry shops are only too pleased to give it away. Shavings absorb the rabbit's urine quickly and efficiently and also provide a layer of warm insulation for the hutch floor, especially useful during the winter months.

The rabbit's sleeping quarters should be provided with a sizeable wad of clean straw as well as the usual floor covering; and be it wheat, barley, or oat straw, your rabbit will build a cozy nest for himself.

It is best to have set days and times for giving the hutch a thorough cleaning, thus ensuring that one gets into the habit and does not forget. Pick two days of the week, say Wednesday and Sunday or whatever is convenient, make a time of say 8 a.m. or 5 p.m., and stick to it. This will also suit your rabbits. They will get used to these regular disturbances, will learn to accept them, and will not be upset.

When cleaning, remove the animals from the hutch and put them in a safe place. Never put a nervous animal on a high table, for if it should fall it could fracture a limb or sustain a serious internal injury. A tame pet can often be placed in the immediate vicinity of the hutch while cleaning is in progress and it will not run away, indeed it will likely be curious enough to show interest in what is going on.

Cleaning equipment may consist of a scraper (the type used for scraping paint is ideal), a hand shovel, a bucket, and a stiff scrubbing brush. Normally it will be sufficient to scrape the soiled covering loose from the floor and then shovel it into the bucket. It is not necessary to scrub out the hutch every time but the occasional, say quarterly, scrub with a solution of disinfectant or household ammonia in warm water will ensure that any germs or parasites lurking in the wood joints are destroyed. The hutch should be thoroughly dried out before the inmates are reinstalled, so it is advisable to have alternative accommodation available while this is taking place.

The litter which is removed from the cage floor should be taken well away from the vicinity of the cages for disposal. The feces of a healthy rabbit will be individual dark grey spheres that are reasonably firm. For instant disposal it is best to burn it; once ignited it will usually smoulder away quite happily. The keen gardener, however, may prefer to store the manure and let it rot down as compost to produce an excellent fertiliser for the flower or vegetable garden. Although wood shavings or sawdust take a long time to rot, rabbit compost is extremely rich in fertilising elements, more so in fact than farmyard manure. The manure is best stored in an area enclosed on three sides and treated with one of the proprietary composting chemicals to produce a first-class compost in a very short period. Keepers of larger numbers of rabbits may even be able to offset some of their expenses by selling some of this excellent compost to other gardeners.

The area around the hutches, whether indoors or out, should be kept tidy and free of litter and other items which may provide food, cover, or nesting materials for vermin. Dry foods should be stored in metal bins, and hay and straw should be stacked under cover on raised racks.

During routine cleaning the hutches should be regularly and carefully inspected for damage which may have been caused by weathering, by the rabbits themselves, or by rodents trying to get into the hutches. Any cracks should be repaired immediately to prevent draughts and leaks.

Some rabbits develop a nasty habit of gnawing the timber of the hutch, and if not checked they could almost completely destroy the hutch. This habit can often be cured by diverting the culprit's attention to something more attractive, a small branch for instance. Freshly cut branches with juicy bark are most suitable, but beware that they do not come from a poisonous tree such as yew or laburnum. The only way to cure a truly compulsive hutch gnawer is to cover the vulnerable parts of the construction with sheet metal, preferably galvanised steel which is the cheapest, most readily available, and easiest to use. The metal can be cut into strips, bent into the correct shape, and then tacked onto the inside framework of the hutch with short, flat-headed nails.

One of the first things to learn is the correct handling of rabbits. Stories that these animals may be picked up by the ears are totally false. Two hands should always be used when picking up a rabbit and one should always be firm but gentle. With the left hand the rabbit is steadied by the ears or by the loose skin at the back of the shoulders while the right hand is placed under the rump or chest for gently lifting the animal. When examining a rabbit it should always be placed on a non-slip surface, if a smooth table is used a sheet of sacking should be placed upon it. Young rabbits are often

An opal dwarf buck. Dwarf rabbits such as this are excellent pets for children, but only if the children are willing and able to accept the responsibility!

more difficult to pick up as they are usually more nervous and flighty. Small ones may be grasped gently round the loins with one hand and steadied with the other. It is advisable to hold the rabbit to one's chest when picking it up as this will make it feel more secure and thus less likely to struggle.

When purchasing a new rabbit it is essential to ensure that the animal is in the best of health; one does not wish to bring disease to one's existing stock by introducing an ailing newcomer, neither does one purchasing their first rabbit want a sick one.

It is advisable to learn what to look for before attempting to inspect a rabbit with a view to purchasing it. Obviously, if one is contemplating breeding show specimens a good example of the preferred variety will be one of the prime considerations in selection. Ability to recognise such an animal is, however, something which can only be acquired after a certain amount of experience, particularly at shows. It is a good idea to go to a few shows just to study the exhibits and watch the judging. One can pick up many useful tips by doing this even if one has never actually kept a rabbit Before purchasing a rabbit the following points should be covered. Look first at the general appearance of the animal. Its fur should be smooth and sleek, not rough and open which is a sure sign of poor condition. Check that the coat covers the body and that there are no bald patches. The body of the rabbit should be firm and there should be no protuberances of bone, particularly along the spinal ridge. The demeanour of the animal is also important; it should be alert, bright eyed, and show an interest in its surroundings. Its forelegs should be straight and its hindlegs tucked well under the rump, not spread out at the side or bent in an unusual angle which may be an indication of rickets or malformation which must be avoided. Watch how the animal moves. Its movement should be lithe and positive, its ears should turn in the direction of each unusual sound, and its nose should be continually on the move.

One of the most obvious signs of ill health when examining a rabbit is a nasal discharge which indicates a respiratory infection. An ear to the rabbit's thorax will also help when investigating the possibility of a congested lung. A lung infection will be heard quite clearly as the animal breathes. A rabbit with a respiratory infection such as a cold or snuffles will often attempt to clean its running nose with its front paws, and therefore a rabbit with damp, sticky front feet is to be avoided.

Next, look at the rabbit's eyes. If they are bright and alert, there is little to worry about here. Dull eyes are a sign of age and discharging eyes are another sign of disease. If either symptom is present the animal should not be purchased.

A rabbit is "sound orientated", which means that hearing is its most important sense. This is why its ears are so large, independent of movement, and have a rather delicate and precise mechanism inside. Such a sensitive apparatus can easily fall victim to infection, so the ears must always be examined carefully before purchase. Any indications of ear canker such as scabs or waxy deposits should be avoided. This disease is extremely infectious and great care should be taken not to introduce it into healthy stock.

5.
Breeding

Although it is very nice to possess a single cuddly pet rabbit, in the author's opinion one cannot achieve complete satisfaction in rabbit keeping until one has attempted breeding. What can be more exciting than the inspection of a first litter or seeing the young rabbits emerge from their nursery for the first time.

Baby rabbits spend most of their time sleeping,
snuggling comfortably in a nest constructed of dried
plant materials and lined with their mother's fur.
Photo by M. Cummings.

Rabbits are not difficult to breed, in fact they are quite prolific—hence the term "they breed like rabbits". A female, or doe, reaches sexual maturity in four to eight months depending usually upon the size of the variety. A Netherland Dwarf, for instance, will be mature in four months and a Flemish Giant will be seven or eight months old before she is ready for mating.

How does one sex a rabbit? In adults this is relatively easy as the male has a very prominent scrotum which is not present on the doe. In younger rabbits this is much more difficult as the scrotum takes some time to become fully developed. It is advisable for two people to be present for sexing, one to restrain the rabbit and the other to manipulate the genitalia. One person should hold the rabbit belly upwards, preferably on a flat surface, with its hindlegs spread apart. The other person applies pressure to either side of the vent until either the penis of the buck or the clitoris of the doe is evident. This can be ascertained by size, a penis being longer than the corresponding organ in the female. Also, the female organ has a much larger aperture. Before breeding a pair of rabbits it is wise to ascertain a few facts. For instance, are they really a true pair? are they of the right breed? are they in breeding condition?

Selection of the correct breed is of great importance, and if one is breeding exhibition specimens the good points of each member of the pair are the prime consideration. Pairings to produce exhibition rabbits are usually either the best doe in a stud paired with the best buck, or else individuals chosen in hopes that the outstanding features of each rabbit in the pair will balance out the slight failings of the other rabbit. There is always an element of chance when breeding and this uncertainty adds to the excitement for most breeders. From experience a breeder will soon learn which rabbits tend to pass their outstanding traits onto their offspring and which individuals, although of very good quality themselves, do not produce quality offspring.

Here's looking at you, kid! This dwarf rabbit appears to be keeping a wary eye on the photographer. Photo by M. Gilroy.

Accurate and complete records should be kept as a basis on which the breeder can make decisions for pairing. These records should include details of the parent rabbits, the birth date of the litter, and the show history of each of the offspring. After a few generations have been bred the breeder will have an invaluable source of information.

In order to bring a newly purchased pair of rabbits into breeding condition it is wise to keep them separate for about two weeks, during which time they are fed a good balanced diet. If the rabbits are mature there should be no problem in achieving a quick mating. Unlike most other groups of mammals, lagomorphs do not come "on heat" only at specific periods but may be induced to do so by a mating gesture from the buck at almost any time of the year, albeit most prolifically in the months from February to September.

It is normally the practice to take the doe to the buck's hutch because a buck is much more likely to perform successfully when he is on his own territory. Mating in rabbits is extremely fast, so do not be unduly worried if the buck seems to fall off the doe after only a few seconds, for this can quite often have been a successful mating.

After mating, the doe is returned to the breeding hutch which is usually of the type already described in the Chapter on housing. There will be a covered area where the doe can build her nest and bear her young. Do not forget the platform onto which the doe can jump in times of stress when her litter becomes too over bearing for her.

Some breeders like to supply the pregnant doe with a nest box as well as an enclosed compartment. In hutches with no enclosed compartment a nest box is essential as the litter must be protected from draughts. A nest box can be made from plywood or planking and will vary in accordance with the size of the breed, but an average-sized rabbit such as an English will make do with a box some 40 cm (16 in) long x 25 cm (10 in) wide x 15 cm (6 in) deep. One of the short sides of the box should have a hole cut into it to allow the doe to enter and leave the box easily. Holes should be drilled in the base of the box and two dowels nailed under the base so that it does not rest directly onto the floor of the hutch, thus allowing for ventilation and keeping the box dry.

Occasionally a doe will build a nest outside the nest box or even in the open part of the hutch. In this case it is wise to put the nest that she has built into the box and position the box over the space where she had built the nest herself. If the doe still insists on building her nest elsewhere it is advisable to keep the hutch partially shielded with sacking and leave her where she is.

The average gestation period for rabbits is thirty days although this may occasionally vary between extremes of twenty-six and thirty-three days. It is often difficult to tell if a doe is pregnant, or "in kindle" as the fanciers call it, until the latter part of the pregnancy. One method that has been suggested is that if the mated doe is reintroduced to a buck about two days after the initial mating the female will violently repel any advances from the male if she is genuinely in kindle. This method is, however, never 100% foolproof. During the latter part of the pregnancy it is fairly easy to ascertain whether the doe is in kindle by palpation. This is the gentle feeling of the doe's abdomen with the fingertips with the object of detecting the embryo young. With practice this becomes very easy, but take heed as too rough handling of the doe during this period will result in the loss of the litter. During the latter part of the pregnancy the doe should be disturbed as little as possible. This will enforce her feeling of security and result in her being more likely to be a good mother when the time comes.

Be sure that the doe has an ample supply of nesting materials. Straw, hay, or wood wool make a good base whilst the doe will line the inside of the nest with fur plucked from her own underside.

Shortly before kindling time do not be unduly worried if the doe goes off her food or if her droppings become soft. This is quite normal and will right itself after the young have been born. At kindling time the doe will require much more water than usual so it is a good idea to check the water dish two or three times a day. A thirsty doe is likely to kill and eat her litter, so make sure this unfortunate result does not occur. An increase in greenfood during the pregnancy is also advised as well as extra root crops such as carrots, all of which go towards helping the doe produce a good supply of milk for her young. In fact, it is not a bad idea to give the doe a dish of diluted milk once a day in lieu of water. These measures can be continued during the nursing period until shortly before weaning.

When it is noticed that a doe is about to kindle it is wise to leave her undisturbed until at least twenty-four hours after the birth. If the nest is then looked at slight movements in the nesting material will indicate that the birth has taken place, as will the slimmer appearance of the mother rabbit.

It is advisable to examine the litter as soon as possible after this twenty-four hour period has elapsed to ascertain that all has gone well. Gently remove the doe from the hutch and give her some special tit-bit to keep her mind occupied whilst the nest is being examined. Before touching the nest the hands should be rubbed in the floor litter to remove the human smell which might upset the doe.

This litter of baby rabbits is five days old. At this stage, they are starting to get some fur (they are almost naked at birth), but their eyes will remain closed until they are about ten days old. Photo by M. Gilroy.

Baby rabbits are totally blind and almost naked at birth. Their ears are remarkably small and, in fact, they do not look like little rabbits at all. The author has often found it difficult to convince onlookers that litters of baby rabbits are in fact rabbits and not rats or guinea pigs.

Any dead babies should be removed at once and the remainder can be quickly examined. It is possible to sex them when they are still without fur by the presence of small white spots which indicate the teats in does. After the fur has grown this is no longer possible, in which case the more conventional method of identification must be used.

Any obvious runts should also be removed and humanely destroyed. Also, if the litter is excessively large it may be necessary to remove one or more. It is better to have fewer rabbits in good condition than a litter of twelve deformed runts. Six is the maximum number a doe should be allowed to raise herself, any in excess of this number can be destroyed, fostered or hand reared.

Fostering is sometimes possible when two does are in kindle at the same time; one may have a litter of eight and the other a litter of four, for instance. In this case two would be taken from the doe with the large litter and given to the other, thus limiting the litters to six each. Fostering should be done as soon as possible after the birth, up until three days of age. Fosterings after this time are usually risky but may occasionally be successful. The safest time for redistributing the litters is definitely when the young are about twenty-four hours old.

As when examining the nest, the does should be removed and given some tasty tit-bit to occupy their minds while the change round is being carried out. Rub your hands in hutch litter and pick up the young from the larger litter which are to be fostered and place them into the new nest. If there is some distance from one hutch to the other, it is best to carry the young in a box lined with some warm, soft material; young rabbits can chill very quickly if left out in the cold for very long.

Once the initial examination of the litter has been completed and any necessary changes carried out, the doe should be left to rear the young on her own and should be disturbed as little as possible. What can be a better parent than the genuine mother of the infant? However, it may sometimes be necessary to rear young rabbits by hand as described later in this Chapter.

The doe will do all that is necessary to keep her new litter in good health. She will keep the nest at the right temperature by adding or removing material as the weather changes and it is therefore wise to see that a little extra nesting material is always available, particularly during cold weather. She will feed her young from her own milk supply at regular intervals. The young know how to find the teats by instinct and will eagerly attach themselves and drink their fill. She will keep the nest clean by removing soiled material and replacing it with fresh, so ensure that the run part of the hutch is kept clean.

As the youngsters feed steadily they will grow plump and their fur will develop rapidly. Their eyes will open after about ten days and within three weeks they should be leaving the nest and running about the hutch floor. If the young leave the nest before they are three weeks old it could mean that the doe is not supplying them with enough milk, so make sure that she is getting a good supply of water and green food in particular. The greenfood will enrich the mother's milk passed onto the youngsters, thus preparing them for their first solid meals when they leave the nest.

An unusual breed, a black-masked Himalayan Netherland dwarf. Photo by M. Gilroy.

Usually the first time that the young rabbits can be thoroughly examined is when they have just left the nest. They must be checked for any abnormalities. One of the most common complaints in rabbits of this age is bad eyes, often caused by the eye failing to open properly after being infected by bacteria. They may be bathed in water in which a few boric acid crystals have been dissolved. A good veterinary eye ointment then applied should cure this complaint completely.

The first few weeks of a rabbit's life are the critical ones as it is some time before the youngster can build up the immunities necessary to help it fight off disease. Therefore, hygiene at this stage is of the utmost importance; hutches should be kept spotless in spite of the fact that they become dirtier more quickly with a large litter running about in them. Food should be regular, clean, and any sudden changes must be avoided. As the youngsters grow the quantity will increase until they gradually want more more to eat than adult rabbits. They must have ample food supplies if they are to grow naturally.

When the young are between six to seven weeks old, this is something best judged by the fancier, they can be separated from the doe. So that the emotional strain is not too great all at once, it is best to remove the doe from the litter rather than the litter from the doe. This allows the youngsters to adjust to being without their mother before being moved into strange surroundings. They can be left in the nursery hutch for a further few days before being placed in stock hutches. If one is going to sell the youngsters now is probably the best time to do so.

Once the young have been sorted out it is time to have a look at the doe. See that she is in a dry, comfortable hutch. Examine her for any sign of ill health, feed her well, and above all let her rest for at least three weeks after weaning off her litter before attempting to mate her again, waiting even longer if she is not 100% fit after this time.

Rabbits are capable of producing several litters of young each year but it is not advisable to allow a doe more than three if she is to remain in top form. There are records of commercially kept does producing up to eleven litters in one season but in such cases the young are usually fostered. Where a particular doe is superb this of course is one method of producing more young in a shorter period without causing so much strain on the parent.

A phenomenon which occasionally occurs among rabbits is a pseudo-pregnancy in which a doe will carry out all the usual nesting activities but will not produce youngsters as the mating with the buck was for some reason or other sterile. Pseudo-pregnancies indicate that a doe is ready for mating if nothing else and an animal in this condition when introduced to a buck is most likely to conceive. The length of time a mother rabbit can be kept as a breeder may vary from variety to variety or even from individual to individual, but three years is an average breeding life. The average overall life span in domestic rabbits is probably in the region of five years, but records of twelve years or more are not unknown, especially in does which have not been used for breeding.

The buck rabbit may be used to serve a doe as soon as he is mature, and if he is receiving a balanced diet, is fit, and is not overweight, he is capable of mating almost daily. This is not usually necessary unless the fancier is producing extremely large numbers of youngsters. The best stud bucks are those which are kept well away from the does and introduced to them for mating at about intervals of fourteen days. Mating then usually takes place in a very short time, often in a matter of seconds.

Occasionally, in cases of the mother rabbit's death or in severe sickness, the litter may have to be hand reared. This is something which takes a lot of time and a great deal of patience although the results are often very rewarding. A hand reared youngster always makes a much better pet than a mother reared one because it loses all fear of its human foster parent. The orphan should be fed at three-hourly intervals with a good milk mixture. A commercial baby food is ideal and this should be mixed at about one and a half times the strength recommended for new born babies. Rabbit milk is highly concentrated compared to that of most other domestic animals so the young must have a highly concentrated artificial food. The milk may be given from a fountain pen filler, an eye dropper, or even from a toy doll's feeding bottle. The size of the aperture is really something which must be worked out by trial and error. In other words, one must try and establish how much milk the rabbit is going to drink in a certain amount of time without causing any discomfort to the animal.

This may appear to be a baby rabbit, but it is not.
The Netherland dwarf has a combination of features
(round body, short legs, short ears, round face) that
make it resemble most baby rabbits even as an adult.
This red-eyed white was photographed by R. Hanson.

Once the correct quantity and concentration of the artificial food has been discovered the baby rabbits should develop at a similar rate as those which are reared by their mothers. By the age of three weeks the youngsters should be encouraged to eat solid foods and to drink from a dish. As soon as they start feeding themselves the "bottle" feeds can be gradually decreased until they are no longer required, just as with a human baby, but fortunately it does not take quite the same length of time.

Below: *These babies are about ten days old and are just starting to open their eyes. However, they will still be totally dependent on their mother for almost two more weeks. At the age of three weeks, they will begin scampering about the cage and will start to accept solid foods as their mother slowly weans them.*

6.
Health

As mentioned in an earlier Chapter, hygiene is one of the most important factors in keeping a stock of captive animals healthy. There are basically two main groups of diseases, communicable (those caused by an organism and capable of being transmitted from animal to animal) and non-communicable (those caused by other factors such as malnutrition and physical injury and not capable of be-

Maybe he looks a little droopy, but this French lop is actually in perfect health. The lagomorph equivalent of a basset hound, this variety needs special hygienic attention paid to its long ears. Photo by R. Hanson.

ing transmitted from animal to animal). Conditions of the latter classification are more easily prevented as correct husbandry is basically all that is required. Often a problem such as an ingrowing eyelash or overlong toe-nails can be treated without much ado, but conditions due to dietary deficiency, i.e. rickets, are extremely difficult if not impossible to treat once they have become established.

The communicable diseases are all caused by parasitic organisms, whether they be viruses, bacteria, protozoa, helminths (worms) or external arthropodic parasites, i.e. mites. They may be spread in one of four ways; airborne, the disease spreading through the air by the coughing and sneezing of the infected individual; excrementary, the disease passing directly onto the food of the victim through the droppings or urine of the infected individual or transmitted by flies from the droppings of the infected individual to the food of the victim; contact, the disease passing from one animal to the other by direct contact; and carrier, the disease being introduced directly into the body of the animal by the bite of an infected parasite. It must be remembered that the rabbit keeper himself is capable of spreading communicable diseases—always remember to thoroughly wash your hands after handling each rabbit that is infected!

It is often very difficult to diagnose a disease in a sick rabbit although signs of ill health are usually fairly obvious. Some of the signs which indicate sickness are general lethargy, hunched up appearance, diarrhea, sneezing, breathing with difficulty, dullness of coat, dullness of eyes, running of eyes or nose and bald patches in fur. These signs are not likely to appear all at the same time—if they did the animal would be very sick indeed. Any of the symptoms may point to a specific disease or group of diseases, but accurate diagnosis is often best left to the veterinary surgeon who will be able to advise on the best methods of treatment. He is also the person familiar with the latest and most effective medicines to be used in animal treatments and is therefore the one most likely to be able to successfully treat a sick pet.

A rabbit which shows any sign of sickness must be immediately isolated from the rest of the stock. It should be taken to the veterinary surgeon and treated as soon as possible. Any mysterious death should be followed as soon as possible with a post-mortem by either a veterinary surgeon or a pathologist to ascertain the cause of death and if necessary advise on methods of preventing the same.

Some of the more common ailments, their causes, and recommended treatments are described in the following list.

Conjunctivitis

This is a reddish inflammation of the eyelid membranes which can be caused by several different organisms but which can usually be cleared up fairly quickly by using one of the excellent antibiotic eye ointments available today.

Constipation

Lack of greenfood and the administration of too many dry feeds can result in this condition. The cure consists of no more than the addition of more greenfood or fresh roots to the diet.

Fleas and Lice

These external parasites not only cause irritation by their blood-sucking habits but can also act as vectors of more serious diseases. Large numbers of external parasites have been known to cause anaemia, emaciation, and eventual death. Fleas and lice are easy to remove using one of the insecticidal dusting powders specially supplied for the purpose.

Heat Stroke

A usually preventable condition which may occur accidentally is heat stroke. The rabbit may have spent several hours in the unexpected hot sun or have accidentally been left in a stuffy travelling box on a hot day. The rabbit will usually lay at length, panting heavily and perhaps foaming at the mouth. The animal should be immediately placed in a cool, shady, well ventilated spot and provided with a dish of cold water and plenty of cool fresh greenfood.

Mange

Mange is caused by mites similar to those which cause ear canker but in this case they affect other parts of the body. It is usually first detected by the appearance of small bare patches on the body of the rabbit which may become encrusted or septic; can be prevented by the occasional dusting of the animals and their quarters with a veterinary recommended miticide.

Overgrown Teeth

Some rabbits are born with faulty dentition which, if left unattended, may result in the rabbit's death. Should a rabbit lose interest in food and not be known to be suffering from some other problem then the teeth should be considered. Sometimes the teeth of a rabbit grow too long when there is insufficient solid nibbling food available. A veterinary surgeon will be able to cut the teeth back to a suitable length and regular attention to this will allow the rabbit to live a normal happy life.

Overgrown Toenails

The toenails of a rabbit that does not have ready access to hard ground or concrete for its exercise may grow so long that they literally curl around and begin to grow into the pads of the feet. It is a simple matter to gently trim the nails back to a reasonable length, but care must be taken to ensure that the blood vessel in the nail is not damaged.

Ringworm

This is a fungus infection which occasionally occurs in domestic rabbits. The appearance of small, circular, raised patches, yellowish or greyish in colour and usually sited around the ears, face, or muzzle is a sure sign of the disease. If left untreated it will spread over the remainder of the body causing loss of coat and condition. The lesions should be washed, the crusts removed, and the area gently painted with tincture of iodine. This should be repeated daily until the lesions begin to heal.

Snuffles

A common disease in the past, snuffles has been mainly allayed by modern methods of husbandry. However, it still occasionally occurs and the symptoms are persistent sneezing, coughing, and heavy breathing accompanied by a thick yellow discharge from the nose. It is still difficult task to treat this contagious disease and it is advisable that the infected animals be removed from the rabbitry as soon as possible. Severely infected rabbits should be destroyed and then incinerated.

7.
Showing

One of the most satisfying aspects of keeping, breeding, and maintaining domestic animals of one form or another is the ultimate success of winning a prize for the condition of the animal which the owner has himself produced. The condition and quality of a rabbit usually reflect on the attitude of the owner and a patient, conscientious owner will more often produce good results than any other.

These Dutch rabbits are being examined by a judge at a rabbit show. As is the case with dogs, cats, and other domestic animals, rabbits are often bred for show competition, and specialty clubs exist to foster the popularity of rabbits as pets. Photo by D. Robinson.

The owner must also be somewhat fanatical towards his hobby before he can enter into the full swing of exhibiting his stock.

The most important factor in bringing a rabbit into good show condition is good husbandry. They should be given a good balanced diet right from the start, kept in hygienic conditions in a draught-proof hutch, and handled regularly. It is important that a show rabbit be docile and accustomed to being handled and not be placed on the show bench as a nervous, flighty animal impossible to judge. The ideal way of getting into routine handling is to lift the rabbit out of its hutch at a similar time each day and place it on top of the hutch or on a table. The animal can then be gently groomed with a soft brush; thus removing any loose hairs and also helping to bring the coat into prime condition. A healthy rabbit should show a nice bloom or gloss on its coat and this is one of the first things a judge will look for. To give a "finish" to the rabbit's fur a piece of soft silk fabric can be used to polish over the coat of the animal for a few days before the show.

There is little point in entering a moulting animal in a show as this would certainly be passed over by the judges. This is one of the drawbacks of exhibiting, one may spend weeks preparing a rabbit for a show and the animal may start to moult just before the big day. This can be extremely disappointing so it is advisable to have one or two "reserve" specimens just in case this should happen to you.

When entering rabbits for shows it is wise to obtain all the necessary information well in advance such as times, dates, and classes, and the animal can then be dispatched with plenty of time to spare before the show begins.

One of the most important items of equipment to the rabbit exhibitor should be his travelling boxes. The rabbits may be obliged to spend quite a lot of time in them and it is imperative that they be comfortable. A rabbit that has travelled in cramped conditions will not be in its best form for showing. Travelling boxes must vary in size, depending on the breed of rabbit to be transported, and they must be strong because they will have to endure quite a lot of handling. A box for a Dutch Rabbit, for instance, would be about 35 cm (14 in) long x 20 cm (8 in) wide x 30 cm (12 in) high whilst that for the larger breeds such as a Flemish Giant would be 45 cm (18 in) long x 30 cm (12 in) wide x 35 cm (14 in) high. The boxes may be purchased or may be constructed at home. Plywood 1 cm (1/2 in) thick is probably the most suitable material for constructing travelling boxes and the cut out parts should be glued as well as pinned together to give a lasting bond. The real handyman will be able to joint his boxes to make them "last forever" and some people even compete in producing the nicest travelling boxes. The boxes should be given a coat of primer, a coat of undercoat, and a coat of good quality gloss paint for lasting protection. The inside of the box may be left unpainted or given a coat of emulsion.

Ventilation holes should be placed at strategic positions in the box and it is wise to cover these with fine gauge wire mesh to prevent ignorant people from poking the rabbits when they are in transit.

Before dispatching the animals the base of the box should be given a thin layer of clean sawdust or other absorbent material and covered with a good layer of loose straw. The animal can be given a little hay and a piece of stale bread or toast so that it may nibble a little on the journey. The box must be well labelled with its place of destination and its place of origin. It is advisable to have a special label holder attached to the outside of the box for this.

A white rabbit standing erect.

Blue silver fox rabbits. These babies are five weeks old and are now completely weaned. This is the best age at which to sell them if they have been raised for commercial sale. Young animals such as these are more "flexible" than older rabbits and adjust fairly well after the minor trauma of moving and being placed in new homes. Photo by M. Gilroy.

When the rabbits arrive at the show they are allocated a pen where they are to stay until called for judging. The entrants can then be given a final polish with the silk cloth and left to the mercy of the judges. At most shows the rabbits will be presented to the judges by stewards but at small shows the exhibitor is sometimes allowed to sit near his exhibit's pen. At the large shows the rabbits are each given a numbered label that should be stuck to the interior of one of the rabbit's ears. At these shows the rabbit is presented by a steward and is known to the judge only by this number.

Do not be disheartened if your rabbit does not win any prizes, the shows are often as much social occasions as contests. You will have a good chance to examine the winners and get advice from the other breeders, most of whom are eager to discuss their hobby with an interested novice.

Facing page: *Who could resist these little charmers?*